CU00651573

MEDITERRANEA
COOKBOOK

MORE THAN 40 HEALTHY RECIPES YOU CAN
EASILY COOK FOR BREAKFAST

Marco Caruso

© Copyright 2021 all rights reserved.

This document is geared towards providing exact and reliable information with regard to the topic and issue covered. The publication is sold with the idea that the publisher is not required to render accounting, officially permitted, or otherwise qualified services. If advice is necessary, legal or professional, a practiced individual in the profession should be ordered.

From a Declaration of Principles which was accepted and approved equally by a Committee of the American Bar Association and a Committee of Publishers and Associations.

In no way is it legal to reproduce, duplicate, or transmit any part of this document in either electronic means or in printed format. Recording of this publication is strictly prohibited, and any storage of this document is not allowed unless with written permission from the publisher. All rights reserved.

The information provided herein is stated to be truthful and consistent, in that any liability, in terms of inattention or otherwise, by any usage or abuse of any policies, processes, or directions contained within is the solitary and utter responsibility of the recipient reader. Under no circumstances will any legal responsibility or blame be held against the publisher for any reparation, damages, or monetary loss due to the information herein, either directly or indirectly.

Table of Contents

INTRODUCTION

Healthy living is a precious luxury that does not come on its own. You have to program it. Nutrition plays a crucial role in providing the body with essential nutrients for growth and development. While some foods are considered healthy and needed in large amounts, others may be excluded from the daily diet.

 This is how a Mediterranean diet works. The Mediterranean diet is the most common type of healthy diet. Studies have proven that people in the Mediterranean region can attribute the secret of a healthy life to their balanced diet and an active lifestyle. Research has also shown that this diet relieves chronic heart disease and increases life expectancy.

Habits today show that most people prefer to eat fried, frozen, or canned foods that contain saturated fat and sugar. In addition, lifestyles often suggest that most people do not take the time to exercise. As a result, with an increased risk of heart disease, diabetes, and cancer, many people are obese and in poor health.

The Mediterranean diet does not reduce the types of foods that we eat. Instead, the diet advises wise choices regarding food. For starters, instead of canned and frozen foods, eat fresh fruits and vegetables.

 The food plan is based on the Mediterranean pyramid diet. According to him, grains, cereals, pasta, vegetables, legumes, beans, fruits and nuts are food items to include in a daily diet. These nutritious products are a rich source of carbohydrates, tissue, vitamins, minerals and protein. The recommended consumption of milk, yogurt and cheese, low to moderate, reduces the excessive intake of saturated fat. Animal meats such as chicken and eggs should be eaten regularly and red meat several times a month. Fish is considered a better choice because it has high nutritional value.

Olive oil provides good fats, responsible for lowering blood cholesterol levels and maintaining a healthy heart. All of these recommendations are in line with a recommendation for a regular diet of the Mediterranean diet. A balanced food intake thanks to an active physical life. This doesn't mean that people haven't found the time to rest in the Mediterranean region. They also used the time to relax and socialize after each meal, unwittingly giving good digestion and health time.

The Mediterranean diet is rich in fresh fruits and vegetables and low in red meat and sugar. The idea of the Mediterranean diet originated in the countries bordering the Mediterranean Sea, where historically people mainly consume berries, nuts and healthy fats.

Diet can aid in weight loss, heart health, and diabetes prevention.

The Mediterranean (also called Cretan) diet is a way of life, not a quick fix. Its primary benefit is that it does not impose strict dietary restrictions, and its central philosophy is to enjoy food and life!

The Mediterranean diet is not necessarily poor and restrictive. On the contrary, the calorie intake from fats is quite high there, but is due almost entirely to olive oil. On this basis, the nutrition is significantly more balanced than with any other diet.

It is not meant to be cured and strongly crowded out, and it is possible to use healthy life sciences,

There has been increasing concern for their health among men and women in different countries worldwide in recent years. Many men and women often paid more attention to their meals, as they were more concerned with their general health. Both men and women make dietary choices to boost their overall health and wellbeing.

Many of these men and women became interested in the Mediterranean diet as people became more aware of their health and nutrition. So, yes, if you're a person who appreciates the food-health relationship, you may have a keen interest in the history of the Mediterranean diet.

Before fully understanding the Mediterranean diet, you have to be mindful that it is more of a philosophy than a single eating regimen. There is no Mediterranean diet popular to all Mediterranean countries around the world. Instead, the "Mediterranean Diet" consists of the foods that people consume together in the different nations of the region.

The concept of a Mediterranean diet derives from the eating habits and patterns of the people who populate Italy, Greece, Spain, France, Tunisia, Lebanon and Morocco. As a result, the Mediterranean diet also includes a huge variety of delicious foods.  In reality, if a person chooses to embrace the

Mediterranean dining scheme definition, or if a person chooses to pursue a Mediterranean diet system, they will have the ability to enjoy a vast range of delicious food.

The diet of the peoples who populated the Mediterranean Sea regions has remained almost unchanged for over a thousand years. Nevertheless, the region's history is full of examples of men and women living longer than similarly situated people consuming alternate diets. Thus, people in the Mediterranean Sea region have enjoyed longer lives at the same historical epoch through the centuries than people in other parts of the world.

Foods and beverages indigenous to the Mediterranean Sea's geographic landmass are at the heart of the Mediterranean diet. In short, the development of the Mediterranean diet and dining pattern developed initially by providential. The region's people ate those foods naturally and understandably and drank those readily available beverages in and around their homes.

Historical elements of the Mediterranean diet scheme

As already mentioned, the diet of the Mediterranean Sea region's peoples has remained essentially unchanged over the centuries. The Mediterranean diet is made up of a plethora of healthy food items including:

- Fresh fruit
- Fresh vegetables
- Low-fat nuts

- Whole grains
- Monounsaturated fat

The Mediterranean diet, used by humans for generation after generation, in a similar sense, excludes or restricts certain foods that are considered harmful in recent research. These foods are less than desirable and include:

- Saturated fats
- Red and fatty meat
- Rich dairy products
- Fatty fish

The so-called Mediterranean diet is the historical evolution of the Mediterranean Sea basin through generations of cultures and civilizations.

Man learns to grow certain plant species 10,000 years ago, domesticates certain animals, ceases to be nomadic and creates stable population settlements, usually in areas with good climate and water.

Nutrition is already expressed in many texts in the ancient civilizations of Babylon and Egypt. We observe foods that should or should not be eaten and one of them is also forbidden.

The basin of the Mediterranean is a crossroads of nations, languages, cultures, and religions. With various eating practices, diets, fasts, ritual meals, etc. Driven by Christianity, Judaism, and Islam.

The Greeks, Punics, and Romans entered the Mediterranean with wheat, vineyards, and olive trees.

The Germans the rice, citrus, eggplant and dried pasta Muslims butter.

American basic foods were imported from America, such as tomatoes, peppers, and potatoes.

Based on a natural balance of fish and vegetable meats, with plenty of fiber, few saturated fats, this slow and continuous sum of products has given rise to the now commonly called Mediterranean diet. Carbohydrates of fast and slow absorption with ample vitamins and unsaturated fats complement minerals and trace elements.

The Mediterranean was the melting pot of cultures and cuisines, where everything was added. As a result, nothing has stood out and the sun and sea have provided the strong diversity and variety It is a healthy, balanced and highly valued cuisine or diet.

Hopkin (English) and Fujian, the 1931 Nobel Prize, found out what the essential components of a complete diet should be, and that there are other components such as vitamins that are part of the diet.

In the early twentieth century, advances in nutrition went faster than other sciences, seeking the population's welfare.

Scientifically today the so-called Mediterranean diet is considered to be an excellent model of the role.

How does the Mediterranean diet work?

A fiber-rich mixed diet with healthy fats and numerous fresh ingredients such as vegetables, Mediterranean salads, fish and fresh fruit should make our body slim. The Mediterranean diet scores with many important ingredients controlling blood lipids and reducing the risk of heart disease. Quite healthy for digestion are vegetables, fruits and salads. The menu includes pasta, pizza, rice, legumes, cold-pressed olive oil, fresh herbs, and garlic.

The Mediterranean diet program is important: take the time to eat. So it is very important to have a slow and comfortable meal. It takes a lot of time for the Southern Europeans to cook and eat with great pleasure. Smart tactic-now studies have shown this as well: slow eating helps you lose weight. Because if you don't take your time, you also skip the natural feeling of satiety on your body and thus eat more calories unnecessarily.

Mediterranean diet also maintains healthy fat metabolism and reduces the cholesterol levels according to studies. Additionally, scientific research shows a positive correlation between the Mediterranean diet and the prevention of Alzheimer's. For example, a US study has shown that foods such as vegetables, fruit, olive oil and the like can lower the risk of Alzheimer's disease.

The Mediterranean diet does not provide for a supplementary sports program. Calorie counting is not the order of the day, either-you can get enough of the right food. It should always be prepared freshly in the best case.

Benefits of the Mediterranean Diet

We've also heard about the Mediterranean diet's advantages. For example, it would help fight obesity and provide our cardiovascular health with fascinating advantages. It has been called one of the best known and most detailed diets.

Often our lifestyle, quicker and with less time to devote to the kitchen and ourselves, causes us to eat inappropriately and with excessive amounts of fats and chemical components that could impact our health.

The Mediterranean diet means a diverse and balanced contribution of natural and conventional items from this region bathed by the Mediterranean Sea, in addition to a particular lifestyle.

Fruits, fruits, legumes, cereals, olive oil as a source of fat, fish, and eggs and poultry are essential in more moderate amounts.

According to the Mediterranean Diet Foundation's website, the Mediterranean diet is "a significant cultural heritage that is much more than just a nutritious, rich, and balanced template." Will you be aware of the advantages of a Mediterranean diet? Continue reading. We'll tell you everything about it!

This is a type of food that includes both the use of healthy ingredients and healthy cooking methods. Due to its inherent characteristics, this is a highly flavored diet rich in benefits for our health. That is why we will talk about the benefits of the Mediterranean diet.

Fight the so-called bad cholesterol

One of the main benefits of the Mediterranean diet is the abundance of seafood, fish, and vegetables instead of the moderate intake of red meat. This is linked to a drop in cholesterol indices.

It is beneficial for the heart

The Mediterranean diet helps to reduce the risk of cardiovascular disease by containing unsaturated fatty acids in combination with nitrates and dietary nitrates.

Nuts, fish oil, olives and avocado contain such fatty acids.

Prevent stroke

Strokes, better known as stroke, are one of the most common clinical conditions today.

The Mediterranean diet significantly reduces the risk of suffering, as it is rich in olive oil and nuts, which prevent stroke. This is in line with the findings of the Center for the Study of Human Nutrition and Aging at Tufts University in the United States and researchers from the Carlos III Institute of Health

Avoid stomach problems

Combined with polyphenols (antioxidant substances) in apples and red wine, green vegetable nitrates function as a gastric defender. It avoids stomach problems such as ulcers and helps to alleviate them if they have them already.

Control of diabetes

Thanks to the low-fat diet and sweetened desserts, the Mediterranean diet helps control type 2 diabetes .

Decreases the risk of Alzheimer's and dementia

In the Mediterranean diet, the egg is an important element. Due to an optimum state of the blood vessels, these food brain functions are improved. Hence, the risk of mental deterioration in people following this diet is rising.

Help against obesity

Adequate food intake, reasonable carbohydrate consumption, carbohydrates, pasteurized or soft drinks, and the inclusion of vegetables, "healthy" fats and proteins enable both weight loss and ideal weight maintenance.

Help prevent Parkinson's disease

The foods on this diet have great antioxidant power, which prevents cell deterioration and reduces the chance of suffering from Parkinson's disease.

Protect the bones

Adequate intake of calcium-rich products helps to strengthen the bones, which helps prevent fractures and bone conditions.

Provides agility

The nutritious foods from this diet favor firmness and muscle strength, which becomes more physical fitness, regardless of age.

Anti-aging

The abundance of antioxidants and calcium and the reduction in the likelihood of suffering from different conditions suggest better physical health and, with it, a healthy, long and productive life.

List of foods for the Mediterranean diet

It is clear that this way of eating is superior to other "diets", but what foods can you eat? Here is a summary of the best choices in each category.

Proteins:

- Chicken raised in the wild
- Beef
- Veal
- Salmon
- Oysters, mussels, crabs
- Capers
- Squid
- Sardines
- Sea bass
- octopus
- Squid

Vegetables:

- Tomatoes
- Peppers
- Onions
- Eggplant
- Cucumbers
- Okra
- Garlic
- Peas
- Potatoes
- Mushrooms
- Broccoli
- Carrots

Nuts, legumes and seeds:

- Lentils
- White beans
- Chickpeas
- Green beans
- Bean beans
- Yellow peas
- almonds
- Porridge
- Pistachios
- Flaxseed
- Sunflower seeds
- Pine nuts
- Pumpkin seeds
- Walnuts
- Hazelnuts

Grains: (must be whole grain, organic and minimally processed)

- Oats
- Rice
- Rye
- Barley
- Buckwheat
- Bulgur
- Millet
- Cous cous
- Polenta

Fruits:

- Apples
- Apricots
- Avocado
- Blueberries
- Cherries
- Tangerines
- Figs
- Grapefruit
- Melon
- Nectarines
- Peaches
- Pears
- Nar
- Olives

Oils, herbs and spices:

- Extra virgin olive oil
- Rapeseed oil
- Avocado oil
- Anise
- Basil
- Bay leaves
- Cloves
- Cumin
- Dill
- Regan
- Mint
- Regan
- Parsley
- Sage
- Rosemary
- Thyme
- Tarragon
- Pepper pool

You will be able to experience tons of benefits with the help of the information and recipes in this book. For example, the Mediterranean diet is low in processed foods and sugar; it helps you lose weight healthily; it improves heart health; it can help fight cancer, diabetes, and depression; it protects cognitive health and improves your mood; and it reduces stress and helps relax.

1. Tramezzini with ham and gorgonzola

ingredients

- 2 slice (s) of tramezzini bread (soft white bread without crust)
- 80-100 g ham (sliced ham)
- 50 g cheese (Gorgonzola)
- 1 pc. Tomato (s)
- some pepper (ground)

preparation

Top half of the ham on a tramezzini bread. Cut the tomato into slices and place on top. Rub the Gorgonzola directly onto it with a coarse grater and distribute evenly. Season with crushed pepper. Top with the rest of the ham and cover with the second slice of bread. Cut diagonally into two triangles with a sharp knife. Serve immediately or store in a cool place wrapped in cling film so that the juicy white bread does not dry out.

2. Tramezzini with dill cream shrimp

ingredients

- 2 slice (s) of tramezzini bread (soft white bread without crust)
- 80-100 g shrimp (pickled)
- 1 tbsp sour cream
- 1 tbsp dill (chopped)
- salt
- pepper
- Tabasco sauce

preparation

Mix the sour cream with the chopped dill, salt, pepper and, depending on the degree of spiciness, more or less Tabasco sauce. Mix in well-drained shrimp and mix gently. Put on a slice of bread, spread the shrimp and cover with the second slice of bread. Cut diagonally into two triangles with a sharp knife. Serve immediately or store in a cool place wrapped in cling film.

3. Truffle egg dish

ingredients

- 100 g shrimp (peeled and cooked)
- 3 egg yolks
- 125 ml milk
- 125 ml whipped cream
- Sea salt (from the mill)
- Pepper (white, from the mill)
- 1 tbsp truffle oil

preparation

1. Whip the milk, cream, egg yolk and truffle oil in stainless steel dishes, stirring constantly over hot steam, until the egg thickens.
2. Roughly chop the shrimp and stir into the truffle egg.
3. Season the truffle egg dish with freshly ground salt and pepper.

4. Spaghetti omelette

ingredients

- 5 eggs
- 150 g spaghetti (cooked al dente, possibly from the day before)
- 30 g parmesan (freshly grated)
- 30 g butter
- 1 pinch of nutmeg (grated)
- Sea salt (from the mill)
- Pepper (from the mill)

preparation

1. If necessary, cook the spaghetti according to the instructions on the packet and strain.
2. Beat eggs in a bowl. Stir in the parmesan and season with salt, pepper and a pinch of nutmeg.
3. Mix in the cooked spaghetti and stir well.
4. Foam half of the butter in a pan and fry the pasta mixture in it without stirring over a moderate heat until golden.
5. Melt the remaining butter on top of the omelette. Turn the omelette and fry the other side until crispy.

5. Croque Monsieur

ingredients

- 2 eggs
- 1 pinch of paprika powder
- 1 pinch of chili pepper (or grated nutmeg)
- Oil (for frying)
- 8 slice (s) of toast bread
- 4 slice (s) of Gryère cheese (alternatively Emmentaler)
- 4 slices of ham (or 8 slices of bacon)
- 200 ml of milk

preparation

1. For the croque monsieur, cover half of the toast with a slice of cheese and ham or 2 slices of bacon. Cover each with a slice of bread. Mix the eggs with milk, paprika powder, chilli or nutmeg in a deep plate.
2. Pour oil into a pan about a finger high and heat. Briefly turn the filled toasts in the egg milk on both sides and bake in the hot oil on both sides over the lowest possible heat and with the lid closed until the cheese has melted and the toasts are golden yellow. Lift out and pat the croque monsieur well before serving.

6. Greek yogurt with honeycomb honey

ingredients

- 500 g yogurt (Greek)
- 150 g honeycomb honey
- 4 figs (fresh)
- 2 tbsp pine nuts
- Cassis syrup (black currant syrup)

preparation

1. Peel the figs, cut into wedges and mix with the yogurt. Roast and chop the pine nuts and mix them into the yoghurt. Place the yoghurt in a bowl and drizzle with a little honey and cassis syrup.

7. Tramezzini with egg and anchovies

ingredients

- 12 slice (s) of tramezzini bread (soft, juicy white bread without crust)
- 6 egg (s) (hard-boiled and thinly sliced)
- 12 pieces of anchovy fillets (pickled)
- 200 g mayonnaise (homemade if possible)

preparation

1. Brush the bread slices generously with mayonnaise. Cover half of the bread with half of the egg slices. Place the drained anchovy fillets on top and cover with the remaining egg slices. Place the remaining bread slices on top and cut diagonally into two triangles.

8. Herb omelette

ingredients

- 12 eggs
- 12 tbsp herbs (of your choice, washed, finely chopped)
- 6 tbsp butter
- 1 tbsp flour
- 1/8 l milk
- salt
- pepper
- 2 tbsp parmesan (or other hard cheese to taste)

preparation

1. The herb omelette melted first in a pan of butter and fry the herbs gently on a low heat. Caution: The herbs must never brown!
2. In the meantime, stir the eggs with salt, pepper, Parmesan, flour and milk into a liquid pancake batter. Pour carefully over the herbs, stir well. (Add a little butter to taste so that the other side is crispy too.) when a firm crust has formed on the underside, turn the dough and finish baking.
3. Arrange the herb omelette on plates and serve.

9. Caprese toast

ingredients

- 1-2 tomatoes
- 2 packs of mozzarella
- 1 clove of garlic
- 4 slices of toast
- 1 tbsp pesto (basil)
- 1 tbsp olive oil
- Basil (fresh)
- salt
- Pepper (from the mill)

preparation

1. For the Caprese toast, first wash the tomatoes and cut them into slices. Next, peel garlic and chop finely. Also cut the mozzarella into slices.
2. Brush the toast slices with pesto and place the tomatoes and mozzarella on top. Mix the garlic and olive oil and spread on top.
3. Bake the toasts with the grill function of the oven until the mozzarella melts.
4. Salt and pepper the caprese toast before serving and garnish with fresh basil leaves.

10. Italian bread rolls ("pane arabo")

ingredients

- 500 g flour
- 300 g water (lukewarm)
- 1 packet of dry yeast
- 1 teaspoon salt (levelled)
- 1 teaspoon sugar (levelled)

preparation

1. Mix flour, yeast, salt, sugar and water and knead well. It should be elastic and not sticky dough. If necessary, knead in some additional flour. Cover the dough and let it rise until it has doubled (approx. 1 hour).
2. Divide the dough into 8 parts and roll them out with a rolling pin into round or oval rolls. Place the rolls on a baking sheet lined with baking paper and cover with a clean kitchen towel and let rise for another 30 minutes.
3. Preheat the oven to 250 ° C.
4. Bake the rolls for about 10-12 minutes. Then, from the 8th minute onwards, check repeatedly that the rolls are not getting too brown.
5. The rolls can be served warm.

11. Eggs alla Saltimbocca

ingredients

- 4 eggs
- Pepper (black, freshly ground)
- 4 slice (s) of Parma ham
- 8 sage leaves (large)
- 2 tbsp olive oil
- 4 toothpicks

preparation

1. Bring water to a boil in a saucepan and cook the eggs in it for 6 to 7 minutes until they are waxy. Let the eggs cool down, remove the shell and cut in half lengthways. Pepper the cut surfaces.
2. Halve the ham lengthways and wrap a strip around half an egg.
3. Wash the sage leaves, pat dry and attach one leaf at a time to the ham with a toothpick.
4. Heat oil in a pan and fry the wrapped eggs over a moderate heat for about 5 minutes until the ham is crispy. Turn the eggs over.
5. Place two halves of the egg on a plate and serve immediately.

12. Greek yogurt with honey, fig and walnut

ingredients

- 600 g Greek yogurt
- 4 tbsp honey
- 200 g figs
- 4 tbsp walnuts (grated)
- Walnuts (whole, for decoration)

preparation

1. For the Greek yoghurt with honey, fig and walnut, first mix all the ingredients and arrange in 4 small bowls. Garnish with honey and whole walnuts.

13. Pear and hazelnut crostini

ingredients

- 4-8 slice (s) of spelled bread (or baguette)
- 3 pears (Good Helene)
- 2 tbsp hazelnuts (chopped)
- 200 g yogurt (Greek)
- 3 tbsp maple syrup
- Lemon balm

preparation

1. First stir the yogurt with 2 tablespoons of maple syrup until smooth. Next, Wash, peel and core the pears and cut into thin wedges.
2. Toast slices of bread or fry them in a pan with olive oil.
3. Brush the bread with yoghurt, cover with the pear wedges and sprinkle with the hazelnuts and lemon balm.
4. Drizzle the remaining maple syrup over the pear and hazelnut crostini and serve the crostini.

14. Bruschetta with mozzarella

ingredients

- 1/4 kg tomatoes (diced)
- 2 cloves of garlic (finely chopped)
- 1 pinch of salt
- some pepper
- 1 pinch of paprika powder
- 1-2 mozzarella
- 1 handful of basil (chopped)
- some olive oil
- 1 loaf (s) ciabatte (cut into slices about the width of a thumb)
- some sugar

preparation

1. For the bruschetta with mozzarella, fry the tomatoes and garlic in a hot pan with olive oil.
2. Season to taste with salt, pepper, paprika powder, sugar and basil and let it steep for another 5 minutes.
3. Place the hot bruschetta on the ciabatta, place the finely chopped mozzarella on top, let it melt and garnish with basil.

15. Greek omelette

ingredients

- 4 eggs
- 150 g feta
- 2 tbsp olive oil
- Oregano (dried)
- Chives (finely chopped)
- Basil leaves (fresh)

preparation

1. For the Greek omelette, pat the feta cheese dry with kitchen paper and cut into small cubes or crumble.
2. Pour oil into the hot pan and pour in the beaten eggs. Then sprinkle the chopped feta cheese evenly over the top.
3. Let it set slowly over a low flame, sprinkle with dried oregano. Divide the omelette in half, fold it up and sprinkle with chives on the plates.
4. Decorate with fresh basil leaves. Serve with bread and salad. Make sure to have a pepper and salt mill ready at the table.

16. Tramezzini with salami and olives

Ingredients

- 2 slice (s) of tramezzini bread (soft white bread without crust)
- 50-80 g salami (sliced)
- 1 tbsp mayonnaise
- 1 tbsp spring onions (cut)
- 40 g olives (black, without seeds)
- salt
- pepper

preparation

1. Mix the mayonnaise with the finely chopped spring onions and season with salt and pepper. Spread on a tramezzini bread. Cut the pitted olives into slices and spread them on the bread. Top with salami slices and cover with the second slice of bread. Cut diagonally into two triangles with a sharp knife. Either serve the tramezzini immediately or wrap it in a slightly damp kitchen towel or cling film to store in a cool place to prevent it from drying out.

17. Tramezzini with prawns

ingredients

- 12 slice (s) of tramezzini bread (soft, juicy white bread, without crust)
- 500 g prawns (small, shelled and cooked)
- 100 g mayonnaise
- 4 tbsp prosecco (alternatively sparkling wine)
- 1 onion (small)
- 3 tbsp chives (finely chopped)
- Sea salt (from the mill)
- Pepper (from the mill)
- olive oil

preparation

1. Finely chop the onion and sweat lightly in olive oil. Add the prawns and fry for 2-3 minutes until they turn a nice pink color. Deglaze with prosecco, allow to cool and roughly puree everything. Fold in the mayonnaise and chives, season with salt and pepper. Spread it thickly over half of the bread and cover with the second half. Cut each bread diagonally into two triangles.

18. Herbal spread

ingredients

- 125 g curd cheese (lean)
- 250 g yogurt
- 1 tbsp lemon juice
- 1 cup (s) of kitchen herbs (mixed, e.g. chives, parsley, dill, basil, lovage)
- 1 clove of garlic
- salt
- Pepper (freshly ground)
- 1 tomato (for garnish)
- Herbs (fresh or dried, for garnish)

preparation

2. First, for the herb spread, mix the curd cheese and yoghurt and stir together with the lemon juice until creamy.
3. Now finely chop the herbs and press the clove of garlic. Mix both with the curd and yoghurt mixture and season with salt and pepper.
4. Wash the tomatoes, remove the stones and cut into cubes.
5. Serve the herb spread sprinkled with the tomatoes and herbs.

19. One pot pasta with green asparagus and smoked salmon

ingredients

- 500 g asparagus (green)
- 200 g of pasta
- 50 g leek
- 400 ml of vegetable soup
- 150 g cocktail tomatoes
- 200 g smoked salmon

preparation

1. For the one pot pasta, wash the asparagus and cut off the woody ends. Cut the asparagus stalks into 2-3 cm long pieces, put the asparagus heads aside. Wash and slice the leek, quarter the tomatoes.
2. Put the pasta, pieces of asparagus (not the heads), leeks and vegetable soup in a saucepan and simmer closed for 10 minutes. Stir now and then.
3. Add the asparagus heads and tomatoes and simmer for another 5 minutes. At the end, most of the liquid should be soaked up. In between, cut the salmon into not too small pieces.
4. Mix the one pot pasta with the salmon pieces, season to taste and serve.

20. Ricotta cake

ingredients

- Butter (for the mold)
- Semolina (for the mold)
- 4 eggs
- 140 g fine granulated sugar
- 1 teaspoon vanilla sugar (real)
- 500 g ricotta
- 130 g butter (room temperature)
- 1 teaspoon orange liqueur
- 50 g semolina
- 125 g raspberries (fresh)

preparation

1. Preheat the oven to 180 ° C top / bottom heat. Grease a springform pan with a diameter of 20 - 24 cm with butter and sprinkle with semolina.
2. Separate eggs. Using a food processor or hand mixer, beat the yolks with 70 g fine granulated sugar and vanilla sugar to a frothy mass.
3. Beat the egg white, gradually pour in the remaining 70 g fine granulated sugar and continue to beat until the snow is semi-solid.
4. Mix the ricotta and butter in a large mixing bowl, then mix in the yolk cream. Mix in the orange liqueur. Carefully fold in the egg whites and semolina alternately.
5. Pour the batter into the prepared springform pan and bake for 40-45 minutes.
6. Let the cake cool down and serve topped with raspberries.

21. Tomatoes stuffed with Chavroux

ingredients

- 300 g of chacroux
- 20 pcs. Cherry tomatoes
- Parsley (finely chopped)
- Chives (finely chopped)
- Olives (green)
- salt
- pepper

preparation

1. Cut the upper third of tomatoes (with stalk) and set aside. Hollow out the tomatoes and allow the remaining juice to drain for a moment. Mix the parsley and chives and the green olives with a fork. Season with salt and pepper and pour into hollow tomatoes. Place cut parts on the tomatoes. Fresh baguette goes well.

22. grilled tomatoes

ingredients

- 4 tomatoes
- 2 tbsp olive oil
- 3 cloves of garlic (peeled)
- 3-4 pcs. Basil leaves
- salt
- pepper

preparation

1. For grilled tomatoes, first cut the tomatoes in half and cut out the stem end.
2. Make a paste from the olive oil, the garlic cloves, basil leaves, salt, and pepper in a mortar.
3. Brush the tomato halves with the spice paste, place on a grill cup and grill carefully on both sides for about 3 minutes. Serve grilled tomatoes.

23. Flaxseed pancakes

ingredients
- 130 g spelt flour
- 2 tbsp flaxseed (crushed)
- 170 ml almond drink
- 1 teaspoon baking powder
- 1 tbsp agave syrup
- 1 tbsp coconut oil
- 100 g berry mixture

preparation
1. Mix all ingredients, except the berries and coconut oil, into a dough using a hand mixer.
2. Place the dough in the refrigerator for about 30 minutes and let it swell.
3. Heat coconut oil in a pan, add the batter in portions and bake.
4. Top with the berries and then serve

24. Avocado Banana Slices

ingredients

- 2 slices of rye bread (whole grain)
- 1 piece of banana (approx. 140 g)
- 0.5-piece avocado (approx. 90 g)
- 1 teaspoon olive oil
- 1 pinch of iodine salt
- 1 pinch of pepper (black)

preparation

1. Peel the avocado, remove the stone, cut the pulp into cubes, and mix with the oil and a little pepper and salt.
2. Cut the banana into slices.
3. Brush the bread slices with the avocado mixture and top with banana slices.
4. Fold it up and enjoy.

25. Avocado berry porridge

ingredients
- 40 g whole grain oat flakes
- ½ avocado
- 80 ml of oat milk
- 20 g blueberries
- 20 g blackberries
- 1/2 teaspoon black sesame seeds
- 1/2 teaspoon coconut flakes

preparation
1. Core and mash the avocado.
2. Briefly toast the oat flakes in a saucepan, then bring to the boil with oat milk and stir in the avocado. Take the pot off the stove and let the porridge soak for about 10 minutes. Then place in a bowl.
3. Wash the blueberries and blackberries and arrange on the porridge.
4. Garnish with sesame seeds and coconut flakes.

26. Avocado ice cream

ingredients
- 1 avocado
- ½ lime
- 60 ml agave syrup
- 125 ml of coconut milk
- a pinch of salt

preparation
1. Halve the avocado, remove the stone, remove the pulp from the skin
2. Add agave syrup and puree
3. Occasionally puree the lime juice and coconut milk. Salt
4. Put the mixture in the ice cream maker or layer in a bowl
5. Put it in the freezer for 30-40 minutes

27. Banana blueberry porridge

ingredients

- 1 piece of banana (approx. 140 g)
- 60 g blueberries
- 50 g oat flakes (whole grain)
- 75 ml milk (low-fat 1.5% fat)
- 1 teaspoon honey
- 15 g almonds

preparation

1. Put the oat flakes, milk and 125 ml water in a saucepan and bring to the boil briefly over high heat.
2. Always stir well so that nothing burns.
3. Let everything soak briefly over low heat.
4. Put the porridge in a bowl and mix with honey.
5. Place the sliced banana and blueberries on the porridge and sprinkle with almonds if you like.
6. Mix and enjoy everything to eat.

28. Banana French toast

ingredients

- 2 slices of toast bread (whole grain)
- 1 piece of banana (approx. 140 g)
- 50 ml milk (low-fat 1.5% fat)
- 1 tbsp wheat flour (whole grain)
- 1 pinch of iodine salt
- 1 pinch of cinnamon
- 1 pinch of nutmeg
- 1/2 tbsp coconut oil
- 1/2 teaspoon honey

preparation

1. Finely mash the banana and mix well with the milk, flour, salt, cinnamon, and grated nutmeg.
2. Turn the slices of bread in it and let them steep briefly on each side (approx. 30 seconds).
3. Place a coated pan with a little coconut oil and fry the bread until golden brown on both sides.
4. Serve with fresh fruit, a little cinnamon and a little honey and enjoy.

29. Blueberry and cinnamon cake

ingredients
- 2 bananas
- 2 eggs
- 1 tbsp psyllium husks
- 120 g whole wheat flour
- 100 ml of water
- 1 teaspoon cinnamon
- 125 g blueberries

preparation
1. Mash the bananas with a fork.
2. Add the remaining ingredients, except for the blueberries, and mix them.
3. Carefully fold the blueberries into the batter.
4. Pour the dough into a loaf pan and bake at 180 ° C for 25-30 minutes.
5. Let the cake cool and then serve.

30. Basic porridge with psyllium husks

ingredients
- 50 g of oatmeal
- 5 g psyllium husks
- 10 g flaxseed (crushed)
- 150-200 ml oat drink (unsweetened)
- 10 g almonds
- 30 g blueberries
- Optional a pinch of cinnamon

preparation
1. Mix all dry ingredients in a saucepan and then add the oat drink.
2. Bring the mixture to the boil and stir now and then.
3. Simmer until all of the liquid has been absorbed and a thick paste has formed.
4. Serve in a bowl and top with cinnamon, almonds and blueberries.

31. Egg muffins

ingredients

- 4 eggs (approx. 230 g)
- 0.25 bunch of chives
- 6 slices of bacon
- 1 pinch of black pepper
- 1 pinch of iodine salt
- 20 g mushrooms
- 2 pieces of cocktail tomatoes (approx. 50 g)

preparation

1. Preheat the oven to 200 ° C and finely chop the chives.
2. Cut tomatoes and mushrooms into small pieces.
3. Now put the eggs in a bowl, season with salt and pepper and whisk.
4. Place a slice of ham or bacon in a muffin tin.
5. Then add the chives to the egg mixture, mix and place in the muffin tins.
6. Distribute the tomatoes and mushrooms evenly on the muffin tins and bake the muffins in the oven for 10-15 minutes.

32. Strawberry and rhubarb compote on rice porridge

ingredients
- 50 g whole grain rice
- 100 ml of almond milk (unsweetened)
- 1 teaspoon coconut oil
- 1 rhubarb
- 50 g strawberries
- 1 pinch of vanilla
- 1 teaspoon lemon fruit juice
- 1 teaspoon almond butter
- 4 almonds

preparation
1. Cook rice according to package instructions.
2. Clean the rhubarb and strawberries and cut them into small pieces.
3. Heat coconut oil in a pot. Add strawberries, rhubarb, lemon fruit juice and vanilla and let simmer briefly.
4. Warm the cooked rice with almond milk and almond butter in a saucepan.
5. Pour rice into a bowl, pour compote over it and garnish with chopped almonds.

33. Strawberry curd

ingredients
- 100 g strawberries
- 60 g quark
- ½ lemon
- ½ vanilla pod
- 10 g xylitol
- 50 ml of milk

preparation
1. Wash, clean and quarter the strawberries.
2. Squeeze half a lemon and pour over the strawberries.
3. Put the quark, xylitol, vanilla pulp, milk and half of the strawberries in a blender and puree until creamy.
4. Then mix the remaining strawberries with the quark.

34. Peanut Butter – Pancakes

ingredients

- 75 g wheat flour (whole grain)
- 50 ml milk (low-fat 1.5% fat)
- 75 ml of yogurt (natural)
- 1 teaspoon honey
- 2 pieces of eggs (approx. 120 g)
- 1 pinch of iodine salt
- 1 tbsp olive oil
- 2 tbsp peanut butter (natural)

preparation

1. Whisk the eggs into a light foam mixture.
2. Mix the milk and natural yoghurt.
3. Gradually add the flour, milk-yoghurt mixture, salt and honey to the eggs and keep stirring.
4. The dough should have a thick consistency.
5. Heat the pan on medium heat and add a teaspoon of oil for each pancake and bake the whole dough into pancakes one after the other.
6. Finally, coat the pancakes with peanut butter and serve.

35. Raspberry French toast

ingredients
- 2 slices of toast bread (whole grain)
- 1 piece of banana (approx. 140 g)
- 50 ml milk (low-fat 1.5% fat)
- 1 tbsp wheat flour (whole grain)
- 1 pinch of iodine salt
- 30 g raspberries
- 10 g almonds
- 1/2 tbsp coconut oil
- 1/2 teaspoon honey

preparation
1. Finely mash the banana and mix well with the milk, flour and salt.
2. Turn the slices of bread in it and let them steep briefly on each side (approx. 30 seconds).
3. Place a coated pan with a little coconut oil and fry the bread until golden brown on both sides.
4. Serve with raspberries, almonds and a little honey and enjoy.

36. Raspberry and Banana Porridge

ingredients

- 30 g whole grain oat flakes
- 10 g amaranth puffed
- 1 teaspoon chia seeds
- 1 teaspoon flaxseed
- 100 ml of mineral water
- 1 banana
- 40 g raspberries
- 10 g cashews
- 1 teaspoon agave syrup

preparation

1. Bring the oatmeal, amaranth, chia seeds and flax seeds to a boil with water in a saucepan, simmer on low heat for about 5 minutes until a creamy consistency is obtained. If necessary, add a dash of water.
2. Mash the banana with a fork and fold it into the porridge.
3. Arrange the porridge in a bowl.
4. Wash the raspberries and pour over the porridge. Garnish with cashews and agave syrup.

37. Cheesecake Pizza

ingredients

- 125 g whole wheat flour
- 5 g fresh yeast
- 60 ml low-fat milk
- 1 teaspoon sunflower oil
- ½ teaspoon salt
- 70 g quark
- 1 egg
- 8 g cornstarch
- some bourbon vanilla flavour
- 1 rhubarb

preparation

1. Dissolve the yeast in the milk. Add flour, oil and salt and knead into a smooth dough. Cover and let the dough rise in a warm place for about 90 minutes. The volume should have increased visibly.
2. For the topping, mix the quark, egg, cornstarch and bourbon vanilla flavour and sweeten with honey to taste.
3. Clean and chop the rhubarb.
4. When the dough has risen, roll it out in a round shape, spread the quark mixture and sprinkle with rhubarb. Let the dough rise for 20-30 minutes. Preheat the oven to 200 ° C.
5. Bake the pizza for about 20 minutes.

38. Crunchy muesli with flax seeds

ingredients
- 40 g oatmeal
- 1 tbsp flaxseed (crushed)
- 10 almonds
- 1 tbsp sunflower seeds
- 1 tbsp pumpkin seeds
- 20 ml agave syrup

preparation
1. Preheat the oven to 180 ° C.
2. Halve the almonds and mix with the other ingredients in a bowl.
3. Spread the mixture flat on a baking sheet lined with baking paper.
4. Bake for about 15 minutes.
5. Let cool down briefly and crumble by hand. Then serve.

39. Pumpkin and coconut porridge

ingredients
- 30 g whole oat flakes
- 4 teaspoons of flaxseed
- 50 ml of oat milk
- 45 ml of apple juice
- 100 ml of water
- 1 teaspoon maple syrup
- 100 g Hokkaido pumpkin
- 1 vanilla pod
- 1 dried fig
- 1 teaspoon pumpkin seeds

preparation
1. Cut the Hokkaido into cubes and cook with apple juice in a saucepan over medium heat.
2. In a second saucepan, bring the oat flakes and flax seeds to the boil with oat milk and water and simmer over medium heat. Add more water if necessary. Stir in the maple syrup and the pulp of the vanilla pod.
3. Chop the dried fig.
4. Arrange the porridge in a bowl and garnish with Hokkaido, dried figs and pumpkin seeds.

40. Avocado Scrambled Eggs

ingredients
- 2 pieces of eggs (approx. 120 g)
- 100 g salmon (slices)
- 1/4 bunch of chives
- 1/2 avocado (approx. 80 g)
- 1 teaspoon coconut oil
- 1 pinch of black pepper
- 1 pinch of iodine salt

preparation
1. The chives should be washed and finely chopped, and the avocado should be cut in half, with the core removed and one half diced.
2. Whisk the eggs together.
3. Add the salmon to the eggs after it has been cut into small pieces.
4. Heat the coconut oil in a pan that has been preheated.
5. Place the scrambled eggs in the pan and cook on low heat.
6. To serve, garnish with chives and avocado.
7. Season to taste with salt and pepper.

41. Vegan tomato spread

ingredients

- 100 g dried tomato in oil
- 100 g sunflower seeds
- 3 tbsp olive oil
- 1 handful basil
- 1 pinch raw cane sugar
- salt
- pepper

Preparation

1. Drain the tomatoes slightly in a colander and cut roughly. Put the tomatoes in a tall container and puree them together with the sunflower seeds, olive oil and 4 tablespoons of water.
2. Wash the basil, shake dry and finely chop the leaves. Add the basil to the tomato spread and stir in.
3. Season the tomato spread with raw cane sugar, salt and pepper. The tomato spread can be kept airtight in the refrigerator for 4-5 days.

42. Blueberry yogurt dessert

ingredients
- 4 rusks
- 250 g whipped cream
- 250 g yogurt 3.5% fat
- 1 tbsp mascarpone
- 400 g blueberries
- 1 tsp cinnamon
- sugar

Preparation steps
1. Whip the cream with 2 teaspoons of sugar until very stiff and fold into the yogurt. Add the mascarpone and stir in.
2. Sort the blueberries. Steam 300 g blueberries covered with 3 tablespoons sugar, cinnamon and 1 tablespoon water for 5 minutes. Then strain through a sieve and let cool down.
3. Roughly crumble the rusks. Divide 1 tablespoon each of the blueberries into 4 glasses. Then layer with breadcrumbs, cream yogurt and 2-3 fresh blueberries.
4. Repeat the process until there are no more ingredients. Finish with cream yogurt and fresh blueberries. Serve garnished with flower petals.

43. herbal tea

ingredients
- 2 mints
- 1 bunch thyme
- 2 tbsp mint syrup
- sugar for sweetening

Preparation steps
1. Wash the herbs, put them in a punch bowl, pour on 1.5 l of hot water, stir in the mint syrup and let it steep.
2. Fill into glasses to serve and sweeten to taste

44. Berry granola

ingredients
- 150 g mixed berries (fresh or frozen)
- 200 g curdled milk
- 1 tbsp sea buckthorn juice with honey (health food store)
- 1 tbsp oatmeal

Preparation steps
1. Carefully wash, sort and clean the berries. Thaw frozen berries overnight. Put in a deep plate.
2. Mix the sour milk with sea buckthorn juice and pour over the berries. Roast the oat flakes in a pan until they are fragrant. Sprinkle the berries with it.

45. Yogurt and salmon ham spread

ingredients
- 2 eggs
- 3 gherkins
- 2 shallots
- 1 apple
- 150 g salmon ham
- 200 g yogurt (1.5% fat)
- 1 tbsp chives rolls
- 1 tbsp chopped parsley
- salt
- 1 tsp lemon juice
- pepper
- 4 oatmeal buns

Preparation steps
1. Hard boil the eggs for 8 minutes, quench under cold water, peel and chop.
2. Drain the pickles and dice finely.
3. Peel and finely chop shallots. Also peel and quarter the apple and cut out the core. Finely grate the apple quarter with the vegetable grater.
4. Dice the ham very small. Stir the yogurt with chives and chopped parsley until smooth and season with salt, lemon juice and pepper. Mix in the prepared ingredients. Serve the spread with the rolls.

46. Fruity mango bowl

ingredients
- 1 piece of mango (200 g)
- 50 g strawberries
- 200 g plain yoghurt
- 20 g oat flakes (whole grain)
- 100 ml milk (low fat 1.5% fat)
- 15 g almonds

preparation
1. Cut the fruit into small pieces and add to the blender with milk, yoghurt, oat flakes, nuts, and mix well.

47. Mango and cranberry porridge

ingredients
- 50 g whole grain oat flakes
- 2 teaspoons chia seeds
- 100 ml of oat milk
- 50 g mango
- 10 g dried cranberries
- 10 g walnuts

preparation
1. Boil whole grain oat flakes and chia seeds with the oat milk until a creamy consistency is obtained. Stir in a little more water if necessary.
2. Puree the mango in a blender.
3. Arrange the porridge in a bowl, garnish with the mango puree, cranberries and walnuts.

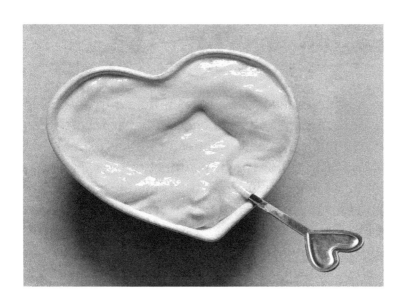

CONCLUSION

The Mediterranean diet has been linked to a reduced risk of cognitive decline. A new study has investigated the claim that the Mediterranean Diet has a long-term positive effect on cognitive function. As a result, scientists have concluded that the Mediterranean Diet is good for the brain. Participants who closely followed the Mediterranean Diet had less cognitive impairment, improved cognitive function, and were less likely to develop Alzheimer's disease than those who did not.

The Mediterranean diet slows down the aging process and helps to prevent bone loss. Researchers presented evidence at a recent conference that a Mediterranean-style diet lowers C-reactive protein levels, one of the main inflammatory markers linked to the aging process. Another benefit of the Mediterranean diet, as shown in the study, is that it reduces the rate of bone loss in people with osteoporosis.

This study found that recommendations for reducing unhealthy foods, such as many industrial foods, halved their consumption among children in this case, were part of the study. Therefore, the Mediterranean diet means reducing the risk of overweight among children, a problem that is growing more and more.

This is a favorable diet to reduce cardiovascular disease. According to the Mediterranean Diet Foundation, eating blue fish at least once or twice a week is very healthy because these fish have fats similar to those of plant origin that protect against heart disease.

The Mediterranean diet is also high in vegetables, greens, and fruits; 5 servings of fruits and vegetables are recommended per day. This provides a high level of antioxidants and fiber, two factors that help to keep these diseases at bay.

This diet is useful for the body to be healthy and the mind is renewed and cultivated. Many doctors and various studies show that the Mediterranean diet improves cognitive functions.

When this type of diet was offered to a group of people for a while, it was shown that they improved their memory and verbal constructions. Foods that improve memory and are part of the Mediterranean diet are nuts, which have omega 3 polyunsaturated fatty acids and blue fish, which have many vitamins and minerals in addition to omega 3.

Some fruits provide vitamin C and green leafy vegetables, they have many antioxidants that are good for the brain. It is clear that we need to vary the different foods in the diet so that we do not always eat them; There is a great wealth of them, so we will not get bored when cooking new dishes.

Everyone should think about how the Mediterranean diet can best be tailored to their lifestyle and personal taste. Then, focus your menu on the foods this diet contains and focus on the foods you like the most.

Sweet treats are not excluded, but they are desirable to consume less frequently and in smaller quantities.

Be physically active by aiming for at least 30 minutes a day or 150 minutes a week. Maintain a healthy weight. Drink alcohol in moderation and give up cigarettes.

PUBLISHER:
KÖRMÖCZI ÁGNES
BUDAPEST, BERCSÉNYI UTCA 60
1192 HUNGARY

CPSIA information can be obtained
at www.ICGtesting.com
Printed in the USA
BVHW061920300821
615612BV00008B/25